VENETIAN MASKS

and the
"Commedia dell'Arte"

arsenale et editrice

Editorial co-ordination
Arsenale Editore

Photography
Archivio Arsenale

English Translation
Peter Eustace

Venetian Masks
and the Commedia dell'Arte

First Edition January 2009

Arsenale Editore Srl
Via Monte Comun 40
37057 - San Giovanni Lupatoto (Verona)
Italy

Introduction

Masks are a *mélange* of truth and deception, sincerity and illusion; their origins are difficult to trace yet, since their exclusively ritual debut, masks have retained over history that transgressive concept that underlies every form of disguise. Queen of the carnival, that knows no distinctions between actors and spectators, the mask ensures a temporary escape from daily life by releasing the more repressed instincts and at the same time highlights human aspects that social life normally denies, revealing at times even certain hidden truths. It is no coincidence that Oscar Wilde, in one of his famous aphorisms, said that "a man is not much when he speaks in first person; give him a mask and he will tell you the truth".

The mask is joined by "dressing-up", a compulsory element of the popular festivals, which thereby celebrates in the form of new garments the people's need to renew their social image. The carnival, unlike official festivals, is therefore a kind of temporary liberation from the existing dominant truth and regime, the provisional abolition of all hierarchical relationships, privileges, rules and taboos. The illusion thus created that every social distinction can be eliminated – impossible in normal circumstances – creates freer and more familiar contact where every lawful language and behaviour is part of general gaiety and collective transgression. Venice, more than any other city, was famed for its carnivals, its unusual costumes and its singular, more or less honest amorous adventures, its more or less fair intrigues – all associated with masks.

Masks and Masquerades of the Venetian Carnival

Mask Workshops

In 1436, the masters of the Guild of Decorators in Venice re-organised the entire corporation by proposing a certain number of orders that were then ratified by the Giustizieri Vecchi – the magistrates responsible for vigilance of arts and crafts. This was when the profession of "maschereri" or "mascareri" (mask-makers) was officially recognised with its own statutes. Growing demand on the market evidently encouraged a significant number of craftsmen to take up a well-established and expanding profession. A document, now in the Correr Civic Museum in Venice, indicates that between 1530 and 1600 eleven craftsmen were registered in this guild as "mascherer" – even including a woman named Barbara Scharpetta. They were joined in their art work also by "targheri" – craftsmen who created new "faces" using not only papier mâché but also fine waxed canvas and, as Grevembroch emphasises, "studied ways to make them transparent, with well-made holes for the eyes, in order to encourage consumption not only in Venice but all over Italy". Inasmuch, mask-making was a customary and common profession – and much more so than one may otherwise deduce from apparent estimates. Despite official recognition of this craft, an historian of the times, Tomaso Garzoni, in his work *Universal repertory of all the professions in the world*, did not disguise his total disapproval of masks as the work of the devil invented with the very birth of mankind. In his condemnation, Garzoni also included the entire profession, which he defined as "dissolute and vain". His moralising arguments against masks and mask-makers are well worth a quotation: "Is there nothing worse than seeing ladies wearing masks and carried piggy-back by Bertoni…? And so many prostitutes dressed like men with legs resembling those of hens? Such dissolution? Such dishonesty? Such obscenities? Such monstrosities? Such pandering incited by their masks? Does not whore-mongering have the same effect? And murders by traitors the same origin?... Some people defend masks, claiming that they are only for enjoyment, a re-creation of the soul, a happiness of the mind, a conso-lation for the spirit, a pastime for gentlemen – but they are truly a deviation of the soul, a digression of the mind, a precipice of the spirit, an invention of ruffians, the brainchild of whoremongers. [...] How better can one visit brothels or hovels than in masks? How better can one mistreat whores than in a mask? How can one speak more clearly and with more trust to housewives and the whores of their husbands?".

Yet masks, according to the same author, even in the midst of so much wickedness, did have something wor-thy: they were useful for political purposes.

"There is nothing good about masks, except that they allow princes to move around in complete safety and freedom and see with their own eyes how their subjects behave, listen to the people's opinions about them, hear praise or criticism, and thus improve matters for everyo-ne's benefit."

Yet the desire to "lose oneself", to hide one's real iden-tity, was much stronger among the Venetians than mo-ralising restraints, and such endless disguises are living testimony of an irrepressible and common desire for li-berty, that regained the loss of identity in a "different" social context, in a generalised expression of happiness that exorcised the faults and evils caused by History.

Mattaccino

The figure of the "mattaccino" already appeared in the oldest chronicles and the first law regulating masks, dated 1268, was entirely dedicated to forbidding the "egg game" that completed this curious disguise. It is suggested that the name derives from the happy-go-lucky "matinees" enjoyed by good-for-nothing young nobles dressed as clowns who used slings to throw eggs filled with rose water towards strolling ladies. They wore lightweight clothes allowing agile movements, at times embellished by ruffs (as we can see in the period engravings and a water colour by Grevembroch). The "mattaccini" were surrounded by crowds of egg sellers, themselves dressed in a bizarre way – resembling, given their strange caps, little devils of temptation. This "game" became so popular that the government, after taking action on several occasions without effect, decided to protect these ladies during their walks by installing nets along the "procuratie" to prevent soiling of their expensive garments.

Even the balconies of beloved women became involved in singular serenades that often culminated in full-scale riots.

Naturally, underhand blows were not excluded – to the detriment of old hags, old wet-nurses or un-amenable mothers, who were struck by the expert slingers with another type of egg having an equally intense but extremely bad smell.

Bauta

The "noble" or "national" mask of the Serene Republic, the "bauta" is the *par excellence* Venetian "disguise" and the most original and typical costume of
the city. This was how it was described in the chronicles of the times:

"She was in disguise, wearing a black silk hood and a
cloak or skirt in silky lace, also black, flowing from her
head – crowned with a three-corned hat –
over her shoulders to cover half her person; this cloak, of course, was the Bauta
and the overall outfit is known as the tabard and bauta masquerade. It was also customary to wear a shiny black or white face
mask… No one recalls the origins of this fashion but, since it is part of the so-called
Bauta with the tabard and three-corned cap, it is probably rather recent."
There is much disagreement about
etymological origins: some experts claim that the term derives from German verb
behüten, meaning to protect, preserve or defend.
Others find affinities
with "*bacucco*" and
"*baucco*" (doddery).
Others still associate
the term with "*bau*"
– a mask used to fri-
ghten children. La-
stly, the word may
even derive from
"*bava*" or "*bava-
glio*" (gag or muz-
zle) similar to the
Piedmont word
"*bavera*" (face
mask).

Yet all commentators of the period agree in defining the "bauta" as the "mask that hides all differences": in short, it was worn by both men and women. It often happened – since these "masquerades" were so similar – that the worst spies and informers, the highest nobility, the meanest populace, the most depraved courtesans, the Doge, the State Inquisitors and foreign princes mingled together as "equals", protected against every insult and offence thanks to the special protection and warranty enjoyed by the "bauta" even as regards the law. Nor should we overlook the fact that the "bauta" added a certain grace to femininity, hid very expensive garments and jewels (forbidden by the "severe" laws against luxury) or even – through fine Burano lacework – offered artful glimpses of otherwise intimate forms. The "bauta" was quite at home at parties, at the theatres, in the coffee houses and for amorous meetings – and was even permitted at times other than the Carnival: in short, it was a garment for all seasons, the elegant protagonist of every important Venetian adventure.

Moretta

The black velvet cap known as the "moretta" was popular with noblewomen and, especially, among less wealthy womenfolk. Naturally enough, it exalted the blonde hair of the Venetians – the pride of women of all classes. Yet is curious to note that this delicate "mask" was also favoured by many men, usually very critical as regards the caprices of female fashions. The reason for this is explained by Boerio in the period itself: "[The "moretta"...] is fixed to the face by a little button held between the lips where the mouth should be".

This mask, inasmuch, meant that wearers could no longer speak – and given the fashion of the time it was accepted by the fair sex.

The "moretta" made its appearance, as seen in many paintings, even among the "casotti" and, during the carnival, welcomed the caprices of mother nature or the marvels brought to Venice from the New World. Inasmuch, dwarfs, giants and extraordinary automatons paraded before incredulous eyes alongside rhinoceroses, elephants, lions and other exotic animals.

Gnaga

The carnival equally offered an occasion to reveal personalities normally "masked" for the rest of the year. The opportunity was taken by young people notified to the State Inquisitors by the vigilant "eyes" of the Serene Republic for their homosexuality. Homosexuality was rather common and attributed by governors to the influence of other peoples, particularly the Turks, who were famous in Venice for this "little vice". Over and above the latter, however, many pranksters found great entertainment by dressing as women. The Venetian "gnaghe" were precisely a mixture of one and the other with an added touch of vulgarity. Some experts suggest that "gnaga" derives from "gnau", the Venetian word for the mewling of cats. The Venetian dialect had a saying: "aver una ose da gnaga" (mewl like a cat) – which Boerio explained as follows: "for a woman, we might say that it means a shrill voice, like that of a flayed cat; and for a man, a harsh or crow-like voice, a voice clucking like a hen or a woman". And to make their interpretations all the more colourful, the "gnaghe" were accompanied by other friends dressed as "tati" or "tate" – dialect terms for babbling babies or very young children: together, with rude and coarse expressions, they roamed around the city bothering all passers-by.

Domino Mask

The "domino" was an elegant variant of the Venetian "bauta", a typical carnival masquerade with a hood. In the second half of XVI century, the French were the first to give this name to the hood used by monks, which later became a common and fashionable garment. Discordance with this origin of the garment comes with the political-religious explanation whereby this particular item of clothing was an act of irreverence as regards the Catholic Church by the English, when the country came into conflict with the Pope.

The origin of the term is a Latin expression of an ecclesiastic nature: *Benedicamus Domino* (Bless the Lord), which returned to Italy through the French.

Larva or Volto

The "larva" or "volto" was a white mask always worn with the classic "bauta". There was even a black version but it was rarely used. Its name is easily traced to a Latin term, the word "larva" indicating ghosts and ghostly masks – a characteristic that was retained over the centuries and well-suited to the gloomy effect it still generates today. They must have seemed truly ghostly under the moonlight in a city lit only by the tiny, flickering flames of the small lanterns of the "codega" – Venetians returning home after a night of revelry at the theatre, in a coffee shop or amidst the gambling tables of an aristocratic casino. Held in place only by a three-corn hat – and thus never removed from the head – the "volto", like the "bauta", was worn by both men and women and, thanks to its particular shape, allowed wearers to drink, eat and breathe freely while maintaining the disguise and at times irritating others seeking "gossip".

The Plague Doctor

The costume originated in France and was "invented" by a doctor in XVI century: Charles de Lorme. The plague in Venice was tragically frequent and reaped it victims at regular intervals. Only two methods were known at the time to ward off its terrible effects: the building of votary temples (Redentore and Madonna

della Salute) and sanitary organisation, still very fragile because of poor medical knowledge. From XIV century, treatises about the plague recommended particular clothing for doctors exposed to the risk of contagion.

The Venetian doctor Troilo Lancetta, who witnessed the tragic plague of 1630, recalled that certain doctors wore "peculiar garments": the tunic was in waxed linen or canvas to prevent contagious stenches being deposited on the clothes of the doctor. A cane was used to lift shrouds without coming into direct contact with infected objects and bodies. Other precautions included a cap, spectacles and that hooked nose, filled with medicinal and disinfecting essences, that turned physicians into ghastly birds resembling ancient witch doctors exploiting ugliness to treat illness. Inasmuch, this was not a carnival costume but the terrifying symbol of a disease which was extremely recurrent in such a maritime city. The carnival embraced this frightful symbol of death to alleviate awareness of such a tragic reality.

Hobgoblins and Elves

The traditional Venetian "zendale" – a short cloak or scarf sometimes tied around the waist or worn on the head by women to go outdoors – was used to create a curious disguise: hobgoblins. The poorest common people, who did not even own a "zendale", used the "ninzioletto", an ordinary headscarf, in its place. The scarf was tied around the neck to create two small horns on top of the head and decorated with ribbons of various colours. Thus turned into little devils – like those common in ancient fairy tales – the women ran through the crowded streets of the city with shrill shouts to frighten other passersby. A simple and innocent pastime just like its popular origin.

The Wild Man (L'uomo selvaggio)

In the century of the "return to nature" and the myth of the "proud native", in the shadow of enlightened civilisation, it is perhaps not so strange to see the re-appearance of a figure boasting a long history. The "wild man", in short, is a rather frequent mask in Italian literature: very hairy, armed with knotty clubs and blatantly wearing animal skins, mid-way between the ingenuous and the hostile because of primitiveness or, by contrast, a lover of the sweet, musical harmonies that Nature, in theory, should have excluded from such ogres – such a figure is the protagonist of many fairy tales. An early representation held in Fra della Valle in Padua in 1208 – "*magnus ludus de quodam homine salvatico*" – is perhaps the most ancient testimony in the Veneto, although mention must also be made of the only '*novella*' in the *Decameron* with a Venetian setting, a terrible manifesto of the innate anti-Venetian stance of the author, as well as certain documents detailing the festival on the Thursday before Lent with figures entirely focusing on this bizarre character.

Chioggia Fisherman (Pescatore chioggiotto)

Playwright Carlo Goldoni famously celebrated the quarrelsome inhabitants of the attractive and wealthy town of Chioggia. A witness to numerous episodes of everyday life that he transposed in his play *Le baruffe chiozzotte*, his work was immediately and hugely successful despite earning him the eternal damnation of the people of Chioggia for making fun of them. Yet the playwright had dryly confirmed that this was merely the truth in the preface to the work:

"Such quarrels are common between humble people and more so in Chiozza than elsewhere; since out of the sixty thousand inhabitants in that city, there are at least fifty thousand of poor and low origin, mostly fishermen or sailors."

In 1791, about thirty years after the first performance of the play, when Goldoni had already settled for some time in France, Venice saw a group of Chioggians form their own acting company and, masquerading as fisher-men, sail their colourful luggers to the Paglia Bridge where they jokingly staged the quarrel that had made them famous all over the world.

A rehabilitation, perhaps, of the "excommunicated" Goldoni? Perhaps it was only a rediscovery of their hot-blooded nature but also, after such sudden ardour, a re-turn to the placid and easy-going dimensions of everyday life.

Bernardon

A libertine city such as Venice, the capital of eros, could hardly not boast a parody as a witness and, at the same time, a protagonist of the indelible signs that carefree and mercenary love may leave on the body. A mask that became an admonition for those entering the kingdom of Venus to taste all its joys without spare.

An old miser, shamelessly exhibiting the ulcers left on his body by youthful excess and the "French disease" that consumed him day by day, hobbled around the city, in the last days of the Serene Republic, singing obscene, trivial and rude songs, barely able to stand on his crutches as he begged. Bernardon was the name of this sinister figure stumbling between the small tables of the coffee bars amidst high-born people: a crude admonition for lazy and profligate youth, so much so that some historians do not exclude the possibility that this 'mask' was inspired by the government with evident moralising intentions – that were naturally ignored. This mask was banned in the period of the Austrian domination.

Children's Masquerades

Children also made their appearance at carnival time: at times accompanied by a "gnaga" or nurse, at others in the footsteps of a clownish Pulcinella making fun with a fishing rod with a sweet as bait to attract their attention.

At other times, they wore fine masks to imitate – with innocence and much more good sense – the behaviour of adults. The carnival was not their only festival; St. Martin's Day on 11 November was dedicated to children. Wearing pure white, long clothes as a symbol of innocence, with laurel crowns on their heads and little drums found in most families, under the protection of their Patron Saint, on the eve of the festival they visited homes and shops seeking pocket money. This tradition still continues today, although no trace of the masquerade remains. The white garments, in short, recall the Saint, the future Bishop of Tours, who, while still a novice and inasmuch dressed in white, gave part of his cloak to a poor and completely naked man.

Sior Tonin Bonagrazia

It is very rare that a personage invented by the imagination of a playwright or an author leaves the stage of make-believe to enter everyday reality: yet the carnival is an utopian place where such things are possible.

Sior Tonin Bellagrazia – an inspired figure created by Goldoni – is the son of a merchant who had purchased, for a modest sum otherwise insufficient to buy a donkey, the noble title of Torcello, who disconsolately left the pitiless public that did not reward him with coveted success to conquer new and greater heights in the main square. With a surname slightly adjusted from the previous, the new Sior Tonin – in real-life Antonio Cagnolini, son of a barber from Cannaregio – tells his attentive listeners that he is a nobleman from Torcello, with endless wealth on the moon and landed estates comprising the shadows made by all the trees of the Earth and the air of which he is the only heir by the wishes of his father.

He shows sparkling gemstones in his hands from the mines in Murano. Short trousers, a three-horned hat and a pigtail complete this living caricature of good times gone by, in an 1800s

Venice that from Queen of the Adriatic had become merely an imperial "colony". Sior Tonin Bonagrazia adapted perfectly and soon won new admirers, ready to hear his quips and Venetian wit. Such a deep mark was left among the inconsolable *laudatores temporis acti* that there was talk of resuscitating the personage, even when no one could be found worthy of interpreting the character, and with the Latin motto *ludere, non ledere* – laugh but do not offend – the parody was transformed in Venice after the unification of Italy into a satirical magazine that in turn left a deep mark on the life and culture of the lagoon city.

The Masks of Farce

The particular "masquerades" of the Venetians should also be joined by some traditional masks for the most part associated with the world of theatre. These naturally only include those well-known in the Veneto-Lombardy area or in any case frequently seen in the Venice carnival.

Pantalone

Pantalone is the best-known Venetian mask. There are no doubts about the origin of this 'mask' since, from its first appearance in the 'Commedia dell'Arte' acting companies, the "first old man", named "Magnifico", spoke in the plain yet musical Venetian dialect. The original name soon gave way to the immortal Pantalone.

There are numerous interpretations about the origin of this name. It is said that it derives from San Pantaleone, one of the Saints venerated in the city, after whom a church is named. Another possible origin is "piantaleoni", a name used for the merchants who opened their stalls in conquered lands and symbolically "planted" the lion of St. Mark to extend the power of the city through trade. The merchant profession in short has strong links with this personage. Others claim that the term is even more ancient and goes back to a Greek expression meaning: "powerful in all things". In any case, it seems to have an etymology prior to the birth of the theatrical mask.

Pantalone is an old merchant, often wealthy and esteemed, at other times completely ruined (Pantalon de' Bisognosi - the 'needy'), yet always an old man in every detail. He shows great vitality in business and energetically and knowingly solving family problems. An often authoritarian father, even to the point of sentimental sacrifice of his sons, he is – together with the "Doctor" – the representative of the conservative class within the scope of the family yet embraces the breeze of innovation among the bourgeoisie in commercial and social fields. His language, at times harsh and licentious, at times becomes more gentle, affable and placid to resemble Goldoni's "gruff benefactor".

The costume involves a Greek-style woollen beret, a red jacket and hose or short sailor-style trousers, with a belt for a sword, handkerchief or bag. He also wears a black cloak, often lined in red, and black slippers, often in the Turkish style with upturned tips.

The black mask highlights some of his physical characteristics: a hooked nose, prominent eyebrows and a curious, pointed beard that he customarily caresses softly with his hands.

The Doctor

A comic personage originally from "well-fed and learned" Bologna. Smart and conceited, a 'doctor' only in name – at times a physician, at others a notary or lawyer – and undoubtedly a figure invented by university students for their theatrical farces. Bologna, a university city boasting ancient traditions, was the ideal homeland of such a character. The 'doctor', like everyone from Bologna, is a gourmet. When called upon to speak, he hides behind his vain "latinorum", mixed with dialect expressions even borrowed from other cities or hyperbolic quotations that as often or not completely miss the mark. Any attempt to interrupt him when speaking is doomed to failure. He dresses in the style of 'doctors': a huge, black suit with a white collar, often with a ruff, and a notary's beret or large doctor's cap on his head. He wears a black mask over half of his face that highlights his bulbous nose and a number of ridiculous warts – a characteristic extensively exploited by many playwrights. Obesity is his particular physical characteristic and comedy precisely plays on the static and heavy nature of this personage. This mask has different names in Bologna: Dottor Balanzone, Balordo or Graziano. Some historians claim that the latter name derives from the Mediaeval jurist famous for his incomprehensible ranting.

Brighella

The shrewd servant in the 'Commedia dell'Arte' or "leading zany", originating from upper Bergamo and thus quite distinct from Arlecchino-Harlequin, the silly and slobbish servant originating from the lower part of the city. Brighella Cavicchio da Val Brembana is his full name.

The etymology perhaps derives from "briga", "brigare" or "imbrogliare" – since tricks and pranks are one of his special characteristics. This meddlesome, greedy and astute servant lives by expedients, a ruffian ready to satisfy even the meanest desires of his master and with the same diligence to turn his back in times of need or danger. He is totally unscrupulous and ready for any craft. He appears as an inn-keeper, sergeant, butler or downright thief. His costume, with several green stripes on a white shirt vaguely recalling a stylised livery, is entirely similar to that of the "zanies", the servants in the 'Commedia dell'Arte' who directly originated this character. At times, he also wears a cloak and a curious cap with green stripes. The mask is black or olive green embellished, depending on the taste of the actors, with other colours. A moustache is a very useful accessory for this personage. He speaks in the Bergamo dialect with singular emphasis. He is an expert musician and often sings when playing the guitar. The fortunes of this character were in part eclipsed by Arlecchino (Harlequin), who became much more popular with audiences – and this why, as the proverb goes, fools write their names in every place.

Harlequin

This is the most popular mask in the 'Commedia dell'Arte', the "second zany" born – it is said – amidst the stagnant air of lower Bergamo and, unlike his countryman Brighella, dim-witted, silly, simple-minded and constantly hungry.

Some experts claim that his garments derive from the *mimus centunculus* of Roman times. Clumsy and always duped, in social terms he stands below Brighella, his trusted friend-enemy and companion in adventures. A drudge and swindler by name and nature, he is always hungry – in the most complete sense of the word – since the actor interpreting him on stage often shared the bitterness of a miserable life. His costume comprises a jacket and trousers with colourful and irregular patches, a white felt beret with a rabbit or fox tail and a belt with a wooden spatula normally used to stir 'polenta' nicknamed "batocio". A black mask covers half the face with devilish and feline features, sometimes with hairy eyebrows and a moustache. He has a puggish nose; all this is set off by a huge bump on his forehead. He speaks archaic Bergamo dialect contaminated by jargon and sayings often borrowed from other cities. Arlecchino-Harlequin is an acrobatic mask involving particularly complex gestures. His swaggering entirely resembles dance. Mocked by one and all, in truth this is the mask most contended by various countries.

Colombina

Colombina is the mischievous and rather twee maid in the 'Commedia dell'Arte', a comic yet not always virtuous figure inspired by the popular world like Arlecchino, her faithful companion in adventures and at times her disconsolate lover. Once on stage, she comes to the fore through her innate gifts of self-assurance, coquetry and typically female artfulness. This character is also known with other names: Arlecchina, Corallina, Ricciolina, Camilla and Lisetta – even to become, in the French fashion, the elegant Marionette in Carlo Goldoni's "Vedova Scaltra".

Her costume is very simple, at times with colourful patches like Arlecchino, set off by a pretty, small white cuff and an apron of the same colour. Other versions entirely resemble the maids of the 1700s. She rarely wears a mask and speaks in various dialects, with a preference for Venetian or Tuscan. Isabella Biancolelli Franchini often acted in this role but it was Caterina, the daughter of the famous 'Arlecchino' Domenico Biancolelli, who gave this figure its particular configuration to leave an indelible mark in the history of theatre.

Pulcinella

The Neapolitan mask '*par excellence*' that originated – despite different opinions – in Campania, a region boasting a wealth of comic traditions. Atella, in short, was the home of farces with the first definitive figures and true masks. Figures such as Maccus, Pappus, Bucco and Dossenus were the inspiration for Pulcinella, often hunchbacked like Dossenus, with a beaky nose like Maccus, a huge mouth like Bucco and the constant hunger of Pappus. Physical features resemble those of a cockerel (the beaked nose was defined by the ancients as *pullus gallinaceus*) and this undoubtedly suggests a possible etymological origin from a dialect corruption of "pullicino" (young chick). Big-nosed, with a squeaky voice, clownish, a failed charlatan, lazy-bones, tumbler and acrobat: this figure appeared in many plots and it was precisely such a 'Pulcinella' that enamoured Giandomenico Tiepolo – who endlessly depicted the character on the walls and ceilings of Villa Zianigo.

The Captain

This mask finds its roots in Roman theatre; mention need only be made of *Miles Gloriosus* by Plautus. A vainglorious, deceitful and braggart soldier inspired by all the adventurers infesting Italy. Yet this figure is also the living parody of the Spanish invader who truly did everything to earn such a damning reputation. The great deeds and extravagant boasting in his language replete with Spanish words – intelligible even to people unfamiliar with this language – acquire the same value as those of Don Quixote.

He wears a bright and colourful uniform: a suit with multi-coloured stripes and gilt buttons, a feathered cap and a frightful sword with several inevitable rust marks or cobwebs – the only trophies he can show for his bloody duels. He rarely wears a mask. His names are always bombastic and terrifying: Capitan Spaventa, Fracasso or Spezzaferro (Captain Fear, Smash or Breaker). Or else recall distant Spanish origins: Matamoros, Sangre y Fuego. He is a demanding lover and often the victim of tricks to which he responds by unsheathing his sword, without ever spilling blood other than his own or that of the actor interpreting the character on stage – wounded by spectators (usually Spanish) displeased by such an offensive parody.

Make-up: Art without Time

Yet Venice is not only comedy and masquerades. Its century-long history offers numerous events narrating the laborious processes needed to create the 'appearances' of everyday life. It soon emerges that while the mask was a way to leave reality behind, even everyday life involved complex preliminaries that reveal dimensions in Venetian social life that are much more modern than we may imagine.

Make-up and Dames

The Venetian 1700s not only involved languid, amorous sighs but also sudden, well-calculated fainting fits, Platonic and Casanovian loves and subtle, yet hypocritical conventions.

Underlying everything there were even inflexible standards for make-up which referred entirely to French fashions. It was against such a background that the high-born aristocracy was joined by another, more recent nobility that soon became the target of the satirical poets: "on becoming rich at the expense of their ancestors – honest, hard-working middle classes and low-born workers alike – the 'new nobility' assumed it could come to the fore, be admired and even overshadow the status of the old aristocracy, enjoying in proud and pointless idleness the wealth amassed through so much effort and so much sweat".

This pleasure-seeking culture saw the emergence of a pretentious and frivolous younger generation that founded its enjoyment on re-born Epicureanism.

Children abandoned to their own devices or mercenary education, marriages used as mere formal rituals, endless lovers and knights who had sheathed their swords to take up the less bloody duels of love were the figures of this world that revolved around women.

It was no coincidence that such a strict observer of behaviour as Abbot Angelo Maria Barbaro thundered:

Gluttony, lust, vice and idleness
Triumph in this Venice
Ripe for an easy remedy.

And this was his proposition:

Take and lock up women at home,
  Women, yes, women,
  Women have overturned
  The laws and virtues of this city.

The women at the heart of such decadence dedicated themselves entirely to the cult of beauty and made the fortunes of the "*muschieri*", the tradesmen who had the exclusive monopoly of perfumes, cosmetics and creams. They were described by Malamani as follows:

"A true lady, how little she may have cared for elegance, nevertheless had to bury herself under a mountain of little bottles of rose water, spirits, essences, alums, oils, vinegars and creams; boxes of gloves and mittens of a thousand qualities from a thousand countries; jars of tooth powders; little boxes for toothpicks and pastilles to sweeten the breath".

Hairdressers – almost all French by birth or convention – became oracles to be questioned and gods of a mysterious Olympus, while homes were converted into full-scale cosmetic laboratories. It was the triumph of rouge, initially imported from Flanders and later manufactured directly in Venice itself – to the extent that certain, unscrupulous and greedy "*muschieri*" soon demanded a production monopoly from the Republic. The abuse of this substance, since it was mixed with mysterious concoctions, caused far from hygienic effects by contributing, on the other hand, to the spread of lice.

Beauty spots soon made their appearance, as well as pieces of taffeta, velvet or satin that women gracefully wore over their faces. There were many different names, at times even rather curious. Depending on their position or shape, in fact, these "black dots" were given singular names: *shameless, passionate, coquette, irresistible, majestic* and even *assassin*. There was no lack, naturally, of criticism and moralising – such as that of an anonymous poet who stated, quite bluntly, that such "announcements" were usually only affixed outside homes for rent. No less caustic was Abbot Seriman in the by no means "imaginary" travels of his Henry Wanton:

"They (these dames) have managed to invent the art of turning defects into something admirable; inasmuch, certain little black 'beauty spots' are added to the face that, if they were natural, would be something vile to be hidden at all costs, and the head is sprinkled with a certain very fine white powder which, by covering the fine black tresses with all the freshness of youth, turn a young head into an old one".

Amidst rouges, scents and other diabolical things, even cosmetics met the utmost disapproval of playwright Goldoni, who explained his reasons very clearly:

"Another custom displeases me. The scarlet red faces of women are so thickly powdered with crimson as to make it impossible to distinguish the ugly from the beautiful or the old from the young, since they all totally masquerade their complexions". The last of these "old tricks" in feminine devilry, again according to another old big-wig, were the hair-styles – which at times, and in all truth, were so exaggerated that even the harshest criticism seems more than plausible:

Women wear such hair styles now
That bring to mind ships' rudders;
There is, alas, no more distinction
Between young, middle or old age.

Twixt artifice and natural curls
Good taste has no proportion –
Since cheeks and chins compete
With hair and its upholstery.

Medusa was not, I think,
As tormented by her snakes
As these dames by their coiffeurs

Pierced with pins, forks and stinking
Insects obliging them to scratch
Even in front of their servants.

Women's heads became hanging gardens involving the most curious geometries and the most extravagant, architectural hair-styles: "Knickknack shops" as Valmaggi said, "here monstrous chimneys, there monumental obelisks and pyramids, here again a rhombus or then again a circle, a square and every other astonishing construction".

They naturally followed the "French fashion" without the least concern for the expense and the sumptuous yet ridiculous result. Meteorologist Giuseppe Toaldo, Professor at the University of Padua, in his essay *On the Venice Bell Tower Electricity Conductor*, referring to the numerous metal arches and castles supporting these "toupees", humorously and ironically suggested that lightning conductors should also be fitted to the heads of these foppish dames.

The Wig and the Beau

Lounger, ladies' man, flirt, admirer, gallant, Parisian and dandy – among other nicknames: the beau, son of the fashions of the libertine century, ended up being the pride of every young beauty or old dame as well as the favourite target of moralists, since the figure represented the frightful gangrene corroding family ties. The role of the beau was described in Bondi's salacious rhymes:

Womanly in dress and manners,
Male only in love's amours,
Neither husband nor bachelor
Yet often both by inclination and craft.

A day-time addendum who dutifully
Keeps company of another's wife,
Skilled by agreement to pass
Entire, long and weary days.

Who reads, if he can, sews and embroiders
And ten hours a day indolently
Serves the shadow or body of his dame.

This strange, indefinable entity,
That amphibious animal known today
All over Italy as "cavalier servente"

Over and above such scandal, the beau's behaviour was wide open to scathing irony. Satire quickly came to the fore and "beau" soon took on very effeminate, emasculated connotations. This phenomenon not only involved the nobility – in short, the *cavaliere servente*' had by then become a common ulcer creeping through all social classes. Contact between different classes in Venice surely helped spread this phenomenon on a massive scale and a quotation by Abbot Chiari, a contemporary and declared enemy of Goldoni, is evident and timely. One of the personages in Chiari's *Chamber Comedies* makes the following point: "And who is not courted by someone in our times? Shop-keepers, flower-sellers, hairdressers and street women would rather go without bread than such a 'servant'. The silliest, ugliest, lowliest, most extravagant and indiscrete are the first to want them and are perhaps still the most fortunate in finding one."

Even Goldoni expressed his opinion on several occasions, always with poor consideration. Pantalone, in *Femmine Puntigliose*, expresses his digust for the fashion of the times:

"You can laugh to death in conversation with women and their *cavalieri serventi*'. There they are, all fixed in adoration; one who sighs over a ribbon, one who kneels to another's lap. One who serves the saucer, another plucking handkerchiefs from the floor. One kissing their hands, one serving their arms, one a secretary, another a waiter, one with perfumes, another who sprays them, one for caresses and another for something more. And the ladies gossip with each other and in agreement tread the men beneath their feet in the triumph of sex over little men reduced to slaves in chains, to worshippers of beauty, idolatrors of such decorum and the scandal of such youth."

The beau first of all had to win the love of his lady's pets and only then could access her court. Soranzo, an aristocrat, even composed a "bestial" little poem – in the fullest sense of the term – dedicated to the bitch of the dame he was courting. The greatest effort, in any case, was to keep up with the current fashion, follow Paris and its new attires and continually re-touch make-up. The beau's day began with long morning sessions attending the toilette of his dame, followed by accompanying her to the hairdresser to offer suggestions or satisfy all her caprices. In revealing their weak constitution, an unknown scandalmonger who published philosophical considerations about these beaus remarked on the need for certain aesthetic and essential appearances:

"many of them still seem to be healthy because of the fine, flourishing colour of their cheeks and lips; in truth, they are not so... these vain effeminates use every means to procure every kind

of ointment and cosmetic to disguise at best their lost handsomeness and thus give a happy impression to the lady they serve." The most pitiable even underwent truly painful treatments, as testified by Dolcetti:

"Venetian effeminates used a thousand recipes to look after their hair … They detested baldness and thereby rubbed their heads with a blend of Spanish fly boiled in oil to the point that blisters formed on their scalps. A few days after such rubbing treatment, it was claimed, the hair began growing again."

In the morning, after grooming themselves and putting on their wigs before going to their dames, some beaus swallowed a spoon of melissa lemon balm and musk to hide every hint of bad breath; a final touch and they were ready to leave and put up with every complaint of their ladies and patrons, to soothe the pains of their ladies' lapdogs and, lastly, openly ready to face the harsh and bitter criticism of their contemporaries.

Brief History of the Wig

Wigs were the essential accessories of perfect beaus and the history of wigs in the Serene Republic is certainly worth more detailed investigation.

The first nobleman in Venice to introduce this French fashion was probably Count Scipione Vinciguerra Collalto in 1668. The lagoon city was literally invaded by this fashion, so much so that the authorities became very concerned. On 29 May 1668, the Council of Ten sought to stall such enthusiasm through a decree that, inspired by such moral laxity, imposed: "it is expressly forbidden that any noble, citizen or subject, of whatever rank and without exception, may wear periwigs or toupees, or any such other items as indicated above and that, within the term of the coming month, in remiss of this absolute decree, offenders shall be subject to the censure of the State Inquisitors."

Yet the reaction was not only decreed by law. The 'opposition' included figures of the calibre of Antonio Correr who, following the decree of the Council of Ten, "created a society of 250 nobles who swore never to wear a wig or encourage such holy sacrilege". This association, however, did not live up to its standards and there were many defections; in the end, only the flag-bearer remained to battle against wig-wearing society. The Government, since no apparent results were forthcoming, decided inasmuch (things never change) at least to benefit from the economic advantages and, following the report prepared by the Magistrate of Ceremonies and, especially, the report by the Superintendents, the Senate announced on 7 May 1701 that "serious and urgent public reasons" justified profit from "arbitrary and luxury items" and "money and income from the universal use of wigs in the City and State" – thereby imposing taxes varying by social class ranging from half a ducat to two ducats. Matters followed their natural course and more wig-makers prospered than ever before; a sign that the Venetians had no fear of laws, decrees or even a tax inevitably far too difficult to impose.

It must also be mentioned that as early as 1435 the "wig-makers" had split from the barbers to create their own school in a site that currently corresponds to n° 4361 in the 'calle' behind San Giovanni Nuovo. Wig styles varied and *The Encyclopaedia of Hair Styles*, published in Venice in 1769, listed as many as 45: the most common were "gropi" (long, curly tresses tied in a knot at the base), "alla cortesana" (courtesan-style with a wide parting falling over the shoulders), "alla delfina" (wavy with a fringe) and "a due bande" (with two plaits). Wigs were made using real hair, cut from living people – although scandalmongers insinuated that it especially came from the poor heads of the deceased. Yet the health problems in the wig trade not only involved such topics but also questions of hygiene. It was only after extensive experiments that G.B. Lucatello managed to overcome such troublesome problems and obtain, with the decree dated 29 April 1763 issued by the Health Superintendent, the privilege of cipria (rouge) production.

The dandy culture of the wig-makers finally won its freedom of expression, even as the Serene Republic began to sink into the dark clouds that soon swept away much more than wigs, rouge and foppish beaus.

The Boudoir of the Courtesan

Among the crafts of human life,
And I think I mean no heresy,
It seems to me there is none finer
Than a women who is a whore.

Every day the usual bell
Opens the door to who know who,
Listening to all this madness,
Who with morning, who with evening winds.

All welcome without deference,
Pulling a little this way, a little that,
And so the purse is always full.

Where in the world is a finer taste?
Enjoy yet make money,
Take the man and dupe the gentleman.

These verses are by Giorgio Baffo (1694-1768), a cultured literary figure and yet perhaps the most licentious poet of Venice, in his definition of the arts and crafts of prostitutes: "the finest trade in the world". Licentiousness was quite at home in Venice and boasted very ancient origins: as early as 1232, laws were passed in an attempt to control prostitution. There even came the time when legislators themselves exploited prostitution itself to combat another widespread custom that in turn was generating even worse problems: sodomy. They allowed prostitutes to exhibit their all their "wares" and "graces" from balconies. This was the origin of the "de le Tete" bridge and quayside in the "Carampane" quarter where these loose women were confined. Initially obliged to live in a part of the Rialto area known as "Castelletto", a kind of ghetto, the "mamole" or common prostitutes were continually granted derogations that soon saw them swarm over other places in the city. This was certainly a full-scale invasion if we credit the 1509 census that estimated the presence of 11,654 prostitutes, more than one thousand of whom were sent to Mestre where the Venetian army was camped. The decree issued by the Council of Ten dated 1480 forbidding prostitutes to "cut their hair short over their faces to disguise their appearance, tie their hair in buns or wear male clothes" was largely ignored – even to the extent that a new fashion emerged, precisely in contrast with these dictates.

Volpi's *Intimate Stories of the Republic of Venice* provide vital information about their ways of presentation:
"It is well-known that loose Venetian women in XVI century dyed their hair blond, as well as their eyebrows, and used make-up on their faces. Such things were forbidden to prostitutes who, on the contrary, went even further. Instead of

rouge on their faces, they placed pieces of meat soa-
ked with milk that they patiently wore for hours on
end".

Another quotation comes from *Habiti antiche et moderni
di tutto il mondo* by Vecelio.

"It is common to find in Venice, above the roofs, certain
square wooden constructions resembling open patios
known as 'altane' (roof-top loggias), where with great
artefice and assiduousness, all or most Venetian women
dye their hair blonde using all kinds of different essences
concocted for the purpose under the great heat of the
sun and with considerable suffering. They sit with a
sponge fixed to the end of a rod that drips to moisten
them. They wear a garment in silk or delicate linen called 'schiavonetto', with a fine straw hat on their heads
against the sun they call 'solana', holding a mirror in
their hands.

After tying their hair up on this broad-brimmed, top-less
cap, and arranging their tresses, the women wait for the
effect of sun-bathing; but what was the recipe?

Many are available in the numerous books about perfumes and ointments, true treasures of cosmetic art, mostly published in the 1500s in Venice. Two very different
recipes are given below – the first from Grevembroch
and the second from Dolcetti's famous text *Perfumery of
the Venetians*:

"Six ounces of alum, four ounces of vitriol, two ounces
of saltpetre, all distilled with water. Honey oil and an egg
yolk mixed together, a blend of vine ash, barley straw, li-
quorice rind, boxwood sawdust and cumin saffron. Finely chopped rhubarb, in a decoction of leaves and
"ghi" shoots, left on a low flame after boiling; then use
a thick sponge to wet the hair, dry with warm cloths,
which is best, and then dry fully in the sun."

And now the other recipe:

"Place in the milk of a woman feeding a male baby a
good quantity of sunflower seeds and then leave for ten
days: then work the mixture with a pestle and press to
squeeze the oil, whose virtues are truly magnificent

when rubbed into the hair, which will resemble fine gold, as well as applied to the face and rubbing well to cleanse for a divine complexion."

Hence the "blonde Venetian", splendour and light in our afternoons, radiant in the masterpieces of so many artists who, evidently, did not only portray courtesans. Yet how many other recipes were there to uphold strict ce-

remonies of love, to maintain the high prestige of courtesans and, not the least to keep teeth gleaming white? Mallow root, boiled in alum with rose water and egg white. Precocious wrinkles were treated with infernal mixtures based on finely ground pigeon dung softened in vinegar, all to celebrate sacrifices on the altar of rouged Venus, transferring entire fortunes to the pockets of the first *"muschieri"* or *"unguentari"*, the makers of cosmetics and ointments with their mysterious bottles and alembics secretly fabricating the eternal illusion of youth for the foolish, as well as serving the foulness of the most vile charlatanry of the vilest charlatans. Yet, when they did not want to resort to the 'masters' of cosmetic art, the courtesans learnt to make shift themselves – as we learn from a passage by Tomaso Garzoni almost evocating the atmospheres of a famous painting by Carpaccio, but not without clearly hinting his total disapproval: "[The courtesans] enjoy beautifying themselves with various creams and rouges, emptying jars of whiting, solimado, box alum, crystal flower sugar alum, sophisticated borraso, giving their skin a shine with bread softened in distilled vinegar, faval water, ox dung water like the cows that they are: and they freshen their faces and soften the flesh with Persico almond water and lemon juice; and they preserve themselves with roses, wine and alum… Here, we see well-prepared mirrors, rose water, nanfe water, musk water, perfumes, civets, ambracano, combs, earrings, broaches, scissors and hair clips. Here again we see boxes, casks, vases, jars, scutellum, all kinds of knickknack and egg shells full of a thousand poultices they prepare themselves. Here we see the knaves prepare 'pomella agucchie', boost their busts, tighten their hips, narrow their shoulders, helping from behind, running forwards, preparing slippers, smoothing out the crinolines and raising their derrieres. Here we see Madonnas with Arab caps, with fringes at the front, with banded horns, blonde tresses, gold belts, broach clasps, diamonds on their fingers, necklaces, long earrings, carnations on the right and roses on the left.

With such genial hairstyles, they sit at the window as rouged jezebels. Nor is this enough since 'elegance' also demands silk gloves, short or long sable cuffs, a lap dog, a kitten at the feet, a monkey on one side, a hammer on the other and a fan close by, all to express extreme lust and licentiousness."

And faced by such a trough of *vanitas vanitatum*, such subtle, erotic artefices to attract and seduce even the most capricious and demanding clients, how can we not reflect on a remark, perhaps by an old libertine at the end of his career and almost at the sunset of the Serene Republic unable to resist the temptation of becoming a moralist:

"all the pleasures of this world are merely vanity but the most vain of all is what should not cost anything yet is bought at great cost and transmitted as hereditary disease".

Contents

Printed in January 2009
by EBS Editoriale Bortolazzi-Stei
San Giovanni Lupatoto (Verona)
Italy